Student's Book

58 St Aldates
Oxford
OX1 1ST
United Kingdom

*Beep Student's Book / Activity Book Level 3*

First Edition: 2014
ISBN: 978-607-06-0940-4

© Text: Brendan Dunne, Robin Newton
© Richmond Publishing, S.A. de C.V. 2014
Av. Río Mixcoac No. 274, Col. Acacias,
Del. Benito Juárez, C.P. 03240, México, D.F.

**Publisher:** Justine Piekarowicz
**Editorial Team:** Griselda Cacho, Rodrigo Caudillo, Diane Hermanson
**Art and Design Coordinator:** Marisela Pérez
**Pre-Press Coordinator:** Daniel Santillán

**Illustrations:** Sonia Alins, *Beehive Illustration*: Jim Peacock

**Photographs:** C. Contreras; C. Pérez; C. Suárez; D. Sánchez; GARCÍA-PELAYO/Juancho; J. Jaime; J. M.ª Escudero; S. Enríquez; A. G. E. FOTOSTOCK/Dennis MacDonald; ACI AGENCIA DE FOTOGRAFÍA/Alamy Images; CENTRAL STOCK; CORDON PRESS/CORBIS/Dann Tardif-LWA, REUTERS; GETTY IMAGES SALES SPAIN/Photos.com Plus, Sonya Farrell; HIGHRES PRESS STOCK/AbleStock.com;
I. Preysler; ISTOCKPHOTO; J. M.ª Barres; PHOTODISC; MATTON-BILD; SERIDEC PHOTOIMAGENES CD;
ARCHIVO SANTILLANA

**Cover Design:** Leandro Pauloni
**Cover Photograph:** THINKSTOCK; iStock

All rights reserved. No part of this work may be reproduced, stored in a retrieval system or transmitted in any form or by any means without prior written permission from the Publisher.

Richmond publications may contain links to third party websites or apps. We have no control over the content of these websites or apps, which may change frequently, and we are not responsible for the content or the way it may be used with our materials. Teachers and students are advised to exercise discretion when accessing the links.

The Publisher has made every effort to trace the owner of copyright material; however, the Publisher will correct any involuntary omission at the earliest opportunity.

First published by Richmond Publishing / Santillana Educación S.L.

Printed in Brazil by Forma Certa Gráfica Digital
Lote: 796878
Cod: 292709404
2024

# Contents

0 Hello!......2
1 Ready for School......5
2 Busy Morning!......13
3 Story World......21
Review 1......29

4 Sports......33
5 Nature Park......41
6 After-School Fun!......49
Review 2......57

7 Transportation......61
8 Summer Fun!......69
Review 3......77

# Hello!

**LESSON 1**

**1** Listen and sing. 0.1

**2** Listen. Ask and answer. 0.2

**LESSON 2**

**3** Listen and sing. 0.3

**4** Draw letters with your finger.

# LESSON 3

**5** Listen and sing.

One, two, three, four, five, six, seven... How many boats can you see?
Eight, nine, ten, eleven, twelve... Come on Robby count with me,
Thirteen, fourteen, fifteen, sixteen... Orange, yellow, green and blue,
Seventeen, eighteen, nineteen, twenty... Pink and red and purple too!

# 1. Ready for School

**LESSON 1**

**1** Listen and sing.

I'm ready for school,
Yes, school is cool!

I have my big schoolbag,
And my sharpener too.
I have my books and my pencils.
How about you?

I'm ready for school,
Yes, school is cool!

I have my favorite ruler,
And my pencil case.
I have my pen and my eraser,
And a smile on my face!

I'm ready for school,
Yes, school is cool!

**2** Tell a friend.

pencil   book   ruler   pen

pencil case   sharpener   schoolbag   eraser

## LESSON 2

**3** Listen and read.

 Hello Karim!

 Hi Lucy!

 Karim, do you have a pencil?

 Yes, I do. Here you are.

 Do you have an eraser?

 An eraser? Yes, I do.

 Thanks. Do you have a ruler?

 No, I don't. Sorry!

 Do you like my picture?

 Yes, it's very interesting!

**4** Ask and answer.

Do you have a blue pen?

Yes, I do.

Do you have a blue pencil case?

No, I don't.

LESSON 3

**5** Listen and identify the pencil case.

**6** Spin and ask a friend.

7

# A School Trip!

LESSON 4

**7** Read and listen to the story.

**Find and Say!**

Now the children are in the snake house.

Look at the monkey, Tom! It's behind you!

But look! The monkey has Tom's sunglasses.

5

It's time for lunch.

I have sandwiches.

I have fruit and yogurt.

Tom! Come down now!

The monkey has Tom's lunch box. The teacher is very angry now.

6

Look behind you, monkey!

Look, monkey! I have a banana.

7

The monkey is in the cage again and it's time to go back to school.

Good-bye, monkey!

Tom, where are your sunglasses?

8

**LESSON 5**

**8** Listen and chant.

**9** Listen and say.

CLIL

**LESSON 6**

**10** Look at the floor plan and count the objects.

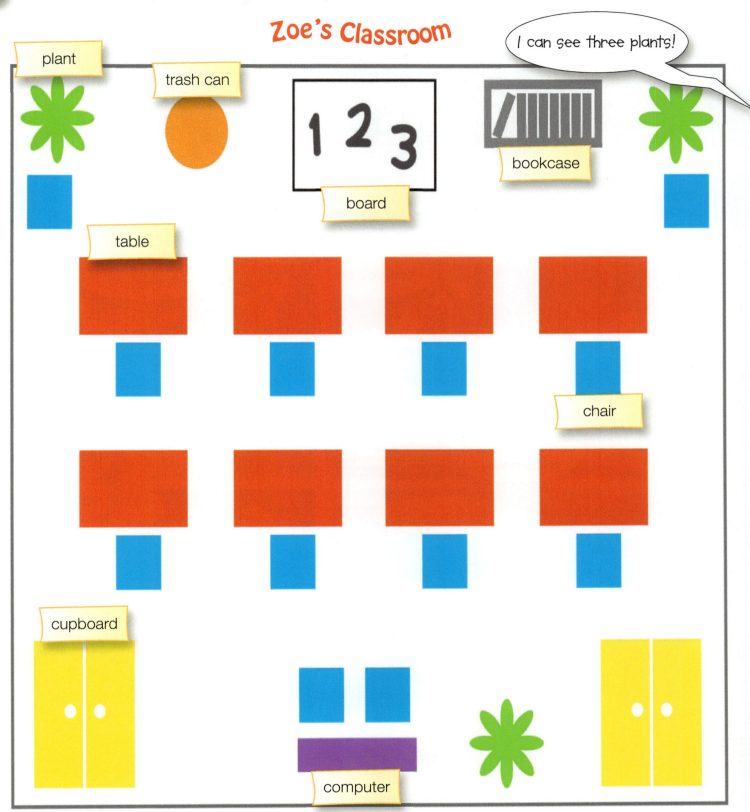

**11** Make a floor plan of your class.

# Beep's World!

LITERACY

**LESSON 7**

**12** Read and listen.

**13** Listen and repeat a tongue twister.

Pink and purple pencils,
Pens and pencil cases,
Peter and Patricia,
Drawing funny faces!

# 2. Busy Morning!

**LESSON 1**

**1** Listen and sing.

Tick, tock, look at the clock.
Busy morning, can't stop.

Get up now!
Brush my teeth!
Hurry up! I'm still asleep!

Tick, tock, look at the clock.
Busy morning, can't stop.

Take a shower,
Get dressed, quick!
Look at the clock.
Tick, tock, tick!

Tick, tock, look at the clock.
Busy morning, can't stop.

Have my breakfast.
Mmm! Great!
Go to school.
Oh no! I'm late!

**2** Listen, point and repeat.

get up

brush my teeth

take a shower

get dressed

have breakfast

go to school

# LESSON 2

**3** Listen and read.

 Hello Olga, get up, please!

 What time is it?

 It's eight o'clock.

 OK, Mom.

 Olga, go to school, please!

 What time is it?

 It's eight thirty.

 OK, Mom, bye!

 Bye, Olga!

**4** Listen, point and identify the clock.

**LESSON 3**

**5** Listen to the lazy prince and point.

**6** Read and say *true* or *false*.

# Lucy's New Watch!

**LESSON 4**

**7** Read and listen to the story.

### Find and say!

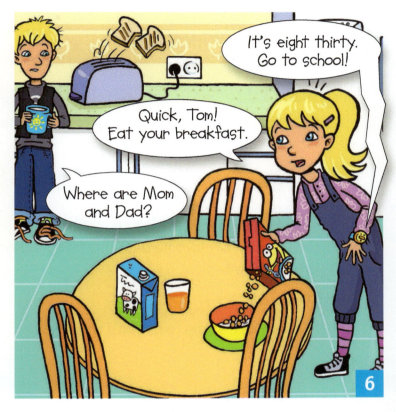

# LESSON 5

**8** Listen and sing.

**Monday, Tuesday,**
I get up and go to school, go to school, go to school.

**Tuesday, Wednesday,**
I see my friends. School is cool! School is cool!

**Wednesday, Thursday,**
Lots to do and lots to see, lots to see, lots to see.

**Thursday, Friday,**
A, B, C and 1, 2, 3! 1, 2, 3!

**Saturday, Sunday,**
Hurray! Hurray! My favorite days, my favorite days, my favorite days.

**Saturday, Sunday,**
NO SCHOOL! It's time to play! It's time to play!

**9** Listen and say the number.

CLIL

LESSON 6

**10** Read and answer.

Hi! My name's Marco.
My favorite day is Saturday.
I get up at ten o'clock.
I ride my bike with my dad in the park.
I have a black bike.

Hi! My name's Emma.
My favorite day is Wednesday.
I get up at seven thirty.
I play basketball with my friends at school.
I like basketball.

**11** Look and say *Emma* or *Marco*.

**12** Ask a friend.

What's your favorite day?

It's Friday. I play computer games on Friday.

# Beep's World!

LITERACY

## LESSON 7

**13** Read and listen. 2.7

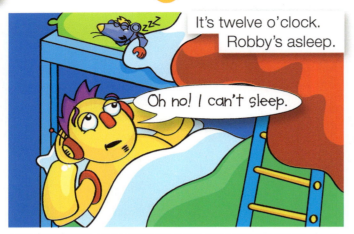

**14** Listen and repeat a tongue twister. 2.8

When Beep can't sleep,
He counts sheep,
Reads a magazine,
And eats ice cream.

# 3. Story World

**LESSON 1**

**1** Listen and sing.

Come to Story World,
Everybody's there.
A prince and a princess,
With long black hair.

A dragon and a witch,
With a little black cat.
And there's a big pirate,
With a black and white hat.

There's a dwarf and a giant,
With his head in the sky,
And look, a superhero!
She can fly!

Come to Story World,
Don't be late.
We love stories!
Stories are great!

**2** Listen, point and say.

superhero

princess

dwarf

prince

giant

pirate

dragon

witch

**LESSON 2**

**3** Listen and read. 🔊 3.2

 Look at the giant. He's tall.

 Yes, and look at the dwarf. She's short.

 Can you see the pirate? He's fat.

 Yes! Look at the witch. She's thin.

 I like the superhero! She's strong.

 I don't like the dragon. He's scary.

 Am I scary, Olga?

 No, Karim. You aren't scary!

**4** Play a game.

**LESSON 3**

**5** Listen and play.

**6** Play a game.

She's tall and thin.

It's the witch.

# Sleeping Beauty!

**LESSON 4**

**7** Read and listen to the story.

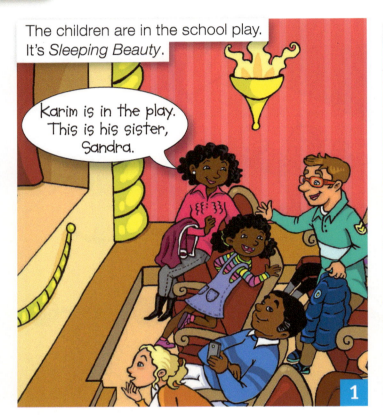

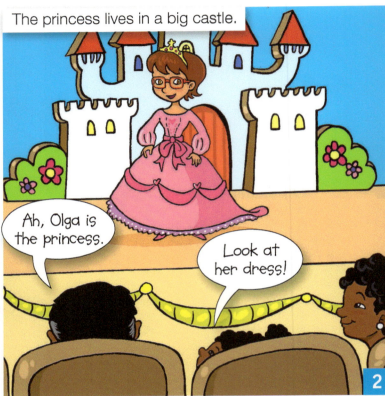

**LESSON 5**

**8** Listen and chant.

This is the witch.
She has a cat.
Her nose is big,
Her hat is black.

This is the princess,
She has a crown.
Her shoes are red,
Her hair is brown.

This is the prince,
And his horse too.
His arms are strong,
His eyes are blue.

**9** Read and say *A* or *B*.

1  Her hair is green.
2  Her shoes are orange.
3  Her cat is white.
4  Her hair is red.
5  His kite is blue.
6  His jacket is purple.
7  His book is green.
8  His jacket is orange.

## CLIL

### LESSON 6

**10** Read and answer.

 Supergirl
 Superboy
 Superinsect
 Superdragon

1. His ears are green.
   His eyes are yellow.
   He is scary.
   What's his name?

2. His legs are thin.
   He is small and strong.
   What's his name?

3. His hair is short and yellow.
   His cape is red.
   What's his name?

4. Her hair is red.
   Her legs are purple.
   She is thin.
   What's her name?

**11** Read and draw.

1. This is Supergirl.
   Her hair is pink.
   She's strong.

2. This is Supermonster.
   He has blue hands
   and legs. He's scary.

# Beep's World!

LITERACY

LESSON 7

**12** Read and listen. 3.5

**13** Listen and repeat a tongue twister. 3.6

Giants like flying kites.
Pirates like riding bikes.
I like climbing.
What do you like?

# Review 1

1. Say!
2. Monday Tuesday ?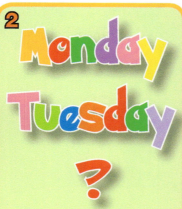
3. What time is it?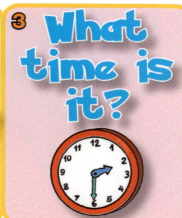
4. Touch a schoolbag!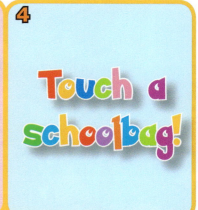
5. Where's the spider?
6. Say!
7. Do you have a white eraser?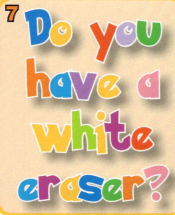
8. Is she scary?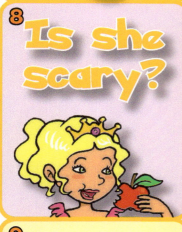
9. Friday Saturday ?
10. What time is it?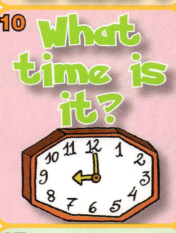
11. Touch a ruler!
12. Say!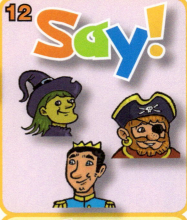
13. Where's the spider?
14. Is he tall?
15. Say!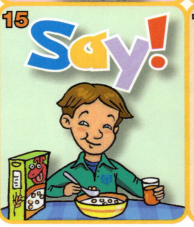
16. What time is it?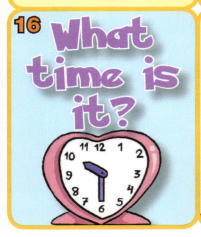

**1** Ask a friend.

1 Do you have a ruler?
2 Do you have a black pen?
3 Do you have a white eraser?
4 Do you have a red pencil?
5 Do you have a blue schoolbag?
6 Do you have a pencil case?

**2** Look and say in pairs.

**3** Say and guess.

# 4. Sports

**LESSON 1**

**1** Listen and sing.

Sports are great!
Sports are fun!
Lots of sports for everyone!

I like tennis. Yes, I do!
I like rollerblading too.
I like riding in the sun.
I like basketball. It's fun!

Sports are great!
Sports are fun!
Lots of sports for everyone!

I like swimming in the pool,
And gymnastics, it's so cool!
I like skiing in the snow.
I like soccer. See me go!

Sports are great!
Sports are fun!
Lots of sports for everyone!

**2** Ask a friend.

Do you like soccer?

Yes, I do.

soccer

gymnastics

tennis

swimming

rollerblading

basketball

riding a bike

skiing

33

# LESSON 2

**3** Listen and read. 4.2

 Do you like photos, Olga?

 Yes, I do. Is this your family?

 Yes, look at my mom. She likes gymnastics.

 Oh yes, but your dad doesn't like skiing!

 No, he can't ski. Look, my sister likes rollerblading.

 Here's your grandpa. He likes tennis.

 And this is my grandma.

 She doesn't like soccer.

 No, she isn't happy. Poor grandma!

**4** Look and say with a friend.

She doesn't like skiing.

Sam    Helen    Joe    Paula

Erica    Greg    Tina    Ben

Tina!

34

**LESSON 3**

**5** Listen and say.

**6** Read and write about a friend.

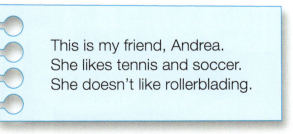

This is my friend, Andrea.
She likes tennis and soccer.
She doesn't like rollerblading.

# School Field Day!

**LESSON 4**

**7** Read and listen to the story.

It's Field Day. Karim is on the soccer team. Olga is in the gymnastics competition. Lucy is in the bike race and Tom is in the rollerblading race.

1

2

Tom has an idea.

3

4

**Find and say!**

# LESSON 5

**8** Listen and chant.

His name's Patrick,
He can do gymnastics.

Her name's Jade,
She can rollerblade.

His name's Mike,
He can ride a bike.

Her name's Kim,
She can swim.

His name's Paul,
He can juggle balls.

Her name's Dee,
She can climb a tree.

**9** Look and say.

Tom can climb a tree.

38

CLIL

LESSON 6

**10** Read and say the race.

sack race

wheelbarrow race

running race

three-legged race

I'm from the United States. Look at the photos of School Field Day at my school.

1 In this photo, there are boys and girls. They're running.

2 In this photo, there are four girls. Look, they have three legs!

3 In this photo, there are two boys and a girl. They're jumping.

4 In this photo, there are two boys. One boy is walking on his hands.

**11** Read and answer.

What's your favorite race?

Can you run fast?

Do you have a medal?

Can you walk on your hands?

39

# Beep's World!

**LITERACY**

**LESSON 7**

**12** Read and listen.

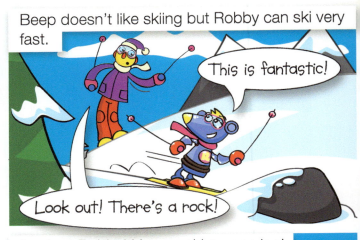

**13** Listen and repeat a tongue twister.

Jane can juggle lots of balls.
Jim can do gymnastics.
John can jump and Jenny can jog.
I think they're all fantastic!

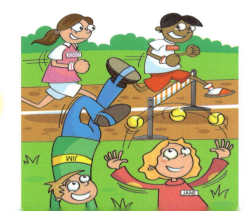

# 5. Nature Park

**LESSON 1**

**1** Listen and sing. 5.1

Come to the nature park with me,
There's lots to do and lots to see.

Animals, animals everywhere,
A big gray wolf, a big brown bear.
There's an eagle in the sky,
Look! A pretty butterfly!

Come to the nature park with me,
There's lots to do and lots to see.

A squirrel climbing in a tree,
Aaargh! A spider next to me!
See the fish in the lake,
Look behind you! There's a snake!

Come to the nature park with me,
There's lots to do and lots to see.

**2** Look and say.

It's big and brown.

The bear!

bear  snake  eagle  spider

wolf  fish  butterfly  squirrel

41

# LESSON 2

**3** Listen and read.

 What's the animal, Karim?

 Does it have legs?

 Yes, it does.

 Does it have wings?

 No, it doesn't.

 Does it have a tail?

 Yes, it does.

 Does it have claws?

 Yes, it does.

 Is it a squirrel?

 Yes, it is! Look!

**4** Play a game.

42

**LESSON 3**

**5** Read and name the animal.

1. It has wings. It doesn't have a tail.

2. It has four legs. It doesn't have wings.

3. It has eight legs. It doesn't have claws.

4. It has a tail. It doesn't have legs.

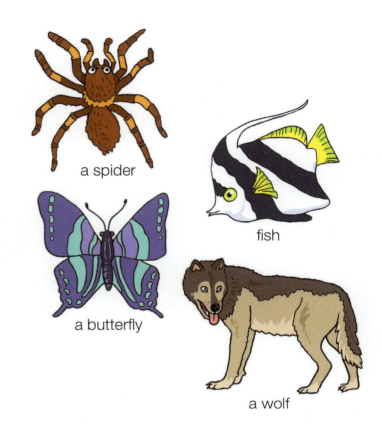

a spider

fish

a butterfly

a wolf

**6** Play a game.

# Bear Attack!

## LESSON 4

**7** Read and listen to the story.

The children are at the nature park.
"Come on Olga. Let's go for a walk."
"Be careful!"

1

Olga can see an animal.
"Oh no! What's that?"
"I don't know. It has a big tail."

2

"Help! It's a wolf."
"Don't be silly, Olga. It's a squirrel."
Look at the squirrel. It can climb very fast.

3

Olga can see something scary with her binoculars.
"Aaargh! It's a horrible monster."

4

**LESSON 5**

**8** Listen and chant. 5.4

A fish can swim.
Oh yes, it can!
A fish can swim all day,
But can it climb a tree?
No, it can't.
No way!

A squirrel can climb.
Oh yes, it can!
A squirrel can climb all day,
But can it fly in the sky?
No, it can't.
No way!

An eagle can fly.
Oh yes, it can!
An eagle can fly all day,
But can it swim in the lake?
No, it can't.
No way!

**9** Read the questions and answer. Listen and check. 5.5

1  Can a bear swim?
2  Can it climb trees?
3  Can it fly?

4  Can a wolf jump?
5  Can it climb trees?
6  Can it swim?

46

CLIL

LESSON 6

**10** Read and match.

1.
It has claws.
It doesn't have wings.
It can climb trees.
It's strong.

2.
It doesn't have legs.
It can swim.
It can't climb trees.
It's gray.

3.
It has wings.
It can swim.
It can't fly.
It's black and white.

 penguin

 tiger

 dolphin

**11** Write and draw.

It has a tail.
It doesn't have wings.
It can climb trees.
It can't fly.

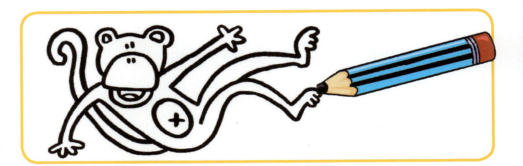

47

# Beep's World!

LITERACY

LESSON 7

**12** Read and listen.

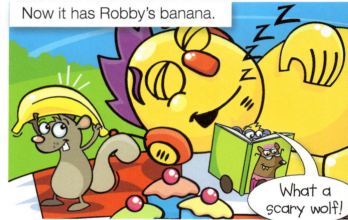
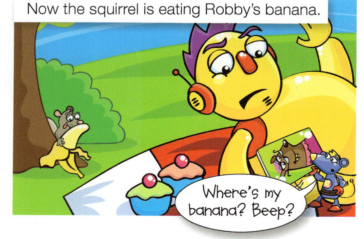

**13** Listen and repeat a tongue twister.

Birds and butterflies everywhere.
But look behind you!
A big, bad bear!
AAAAARGH! What a scare!

# 6. After-School Fun!

**LESSON 1**

**1** Listen and sing. 6.1

After school there's lots to do,
Lots to do, lots to do.
After school there's lots to do,
Lots of fun for me and you!

I like making models,
And I like playing cards.

I like doing puzzles,
And playing the guitar.

I like singing songs,
And I like dancing too.

I like gardening, I like reading.
How about you?

After school there's lots to do,
Lots to do, lots to do.
After school there's lots to do,
Lots of fun for me and you!

**2** Mime and say.

making models

playing cards

singing

dancing

gardening

reading

playing the guitar

doing puzzles

Reading!

## LESSON 2

**3** Listen, point and say the name.

**4** Look and say.

# LESSON 3

**5** Listen and read. 6.3

 Tom, what's Grandpa doing?
 He's making models.
 What's Mom doing?
 She's playing the guitar.
 What's Grandma doing?
 She's doing a puzzle.
 And Dad? What's Dad doing?
 He's reading. And what are you doing?
 I'm drawing you!

**6** Ask, follow and say.

What's Karim doing?

He's doing a puzzle.

Lucy    Karim    Pat    Olga    Emma    Tom

# Where are they?

**LESSON 4**

**7** Read and listen to the story.

Find and say!

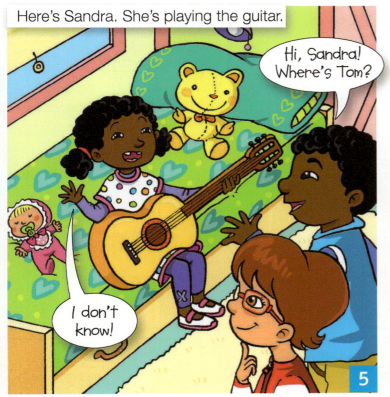

Here's Sandra. She's playing the guitar.
Hi, Sandra! Where's Tom?
I don't know!

Here's Grandpa. He's playing cards.
Hi, Grandpa! Where's Tom?
He's in the kitchen.

Oh no! They can't find Tom!
I'm bored! Let's have some cookies.

It's Tom! He's in the cupboard.
He's eating all the cookies!

# LESSON 5

**8** Listen and chant.

Where's Dad?
He's in the bathroom.
Where's Mom?
She's in the car.
Where's Sandra?
She's in her bedroom,
Playing the guitar!

Where's Grandma?
She's in the kitchen.
Where's Grandpa?
He's in the hall.
Where's Karim?
He's in the garden,
Playing basketball!

**9** Look and ask.

CLIL

## LESSON 6

**10** Read and say the number.

- I like doing puzzles.
- I like dancing.
- I like gardening.
- I like making models.
- I like playing cards.
- I like playing the guitar.

1

2

3

4

5

6

**11** Write about your hobbies.

# Beep's World!

LITERACY

LESSON 7

**12** Read and listen. 6.6

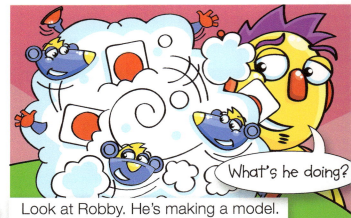

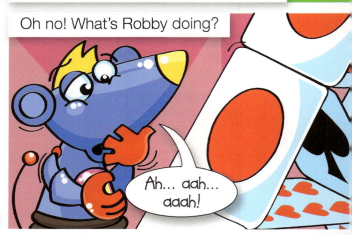

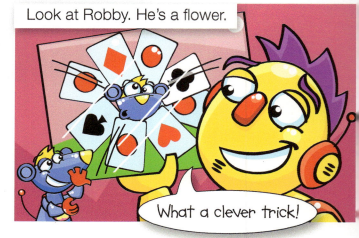

**13** Listen and repeat a tongue twister. 6.7

Gordon's good at gardening.
Gail's good at guitar.
But Gary's good at playing golf.
He's a superstar!

# Review 2

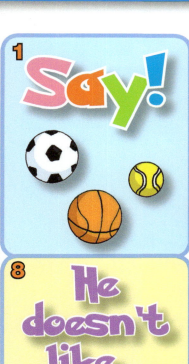
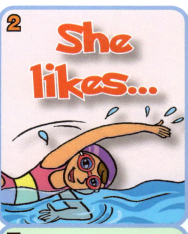
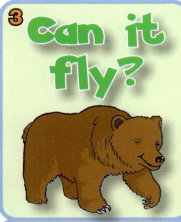

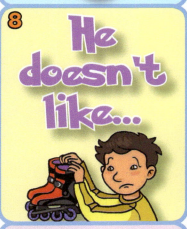

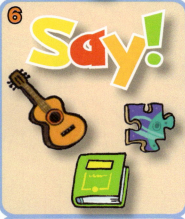
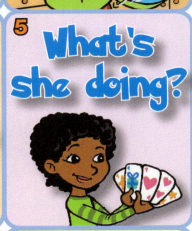

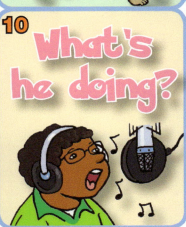

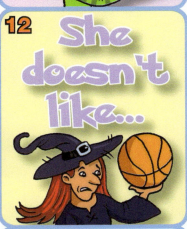
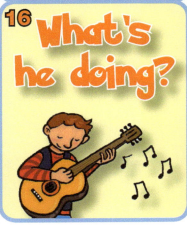
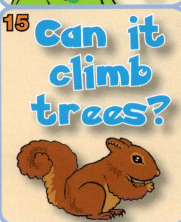
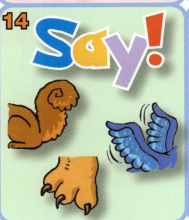
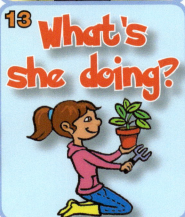

**1** Look and say *true* or *false*.

1 He likes tennis.
2 She doesn't like riding a bike.
3 She likes swimming.
4 He likes soccer.
5 She likes rollerblading.
6 He doesn't like swimming.

**2** Ask in pairs.

✓ = Yes, it does.
✗ = No, it doesn't.

1 Does it have wings?
2 Does it have legs?
3 Does it have a tail?
4 Does it have claws?

**3** Look and say in pairs.

60

# 7. Transportation

**LESSON 1**

**1** Listen and sing. 7.1

Traveling, traveling everywhere,
A bus and a train to get you there.

Traveling, traveling on the sea,
A big, big ship and a boat for me.

Traveling, traveling in the sky,
A plane and a helicopter flying high.

Traveling, traveling on the street,
A bike and a car and my two feet.

**2** Say and spell.

How do you spell boat?

B-O-A-T.

car   boat   helicopter   train

bus   bike   ship   plane

61

## LESSON 2

**3** Listen, point and say.

**4** Spin and say.

**LESSON 3**

**5** Listen and read. 7.3

 Is your car old?
 No, it isn't. It's new!
 Is it slow?
 No, it isn't.
 Oh! Is it fast?
 Yes, it is.
 Is it big?
 No, it isn't. It's small.
 Is your car green?
 Yes, it is! Do you like it?

**6** Ask and say.

# The Lighthouse!

**LESSON 4**

**7** Read and listen to the story.

The children are visiting a lighthouse today.

Quick, Tom. Get off the bus now!

1

The boat is arriving at the lighthouse.

Wow! Look at the helicopter.

Look, there's the lighthouse keeper!

2

When it's night, the ships can see the light.

Hey, Olga, look!

3

Karim and Olga are going up the stairs.

Let's go and see the light!

4

**Find and say!**

 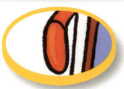    

**LESSON 5**

**8** Listen and chant.

Ten, twenty,

Racing cars.

Thirty, forty,

Going far!

Fifty, sixty,

Fast and slow.

Seventy, eighty,

See them go!

Ninety and a hundred,

Little racing cars.

**9** Play a game.

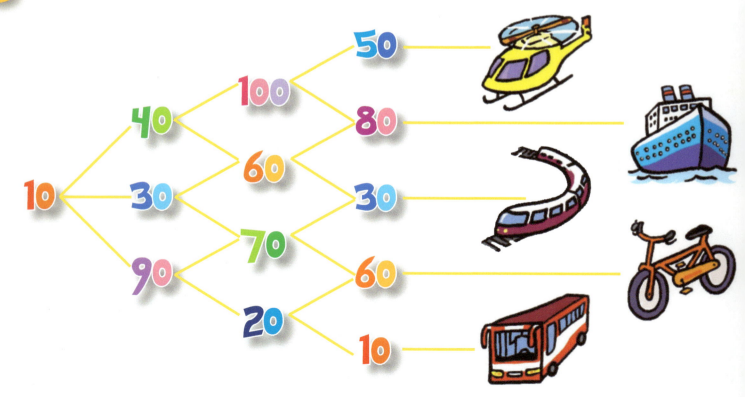

66

## CLIL

### LESSON 6

**10** Listen, point and indicate the hot-air balloon.

**11** Read and predict. Then listen to the answer. 7.6

1. Can children fly in hot-air balloons?
2. Can hot-air balloons fly in the rain?
3. Can hot-air balloons fly at night?
4. Can hot-air balloons go fast?

# Beep's World!

LITERACY

LESSON 7

**12** Read and listen. 7.7

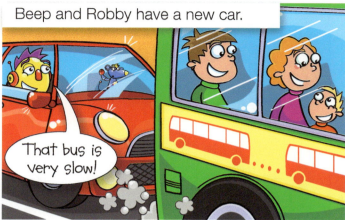

**13** Listen and repeat a tongue twister. 7.8

Trevor travels by tractor.
Trudy travels by plane.
But my friends Travis and Tracy,
Like to travel by train.

# 8. Summer Fun!

**LESSON 1**

**1** Listen and sing.

Summer, summer, summer fun,
Lots of fun for everyone!

We like camping by the sea,
And playing Frisbee®, you and me!

Summer, summer, summer fun,
Lots of fun for everyone!

Sailing, surfing, snorkeling too,
Eating ice cream, me and you!

Summer, summer, summer fun,
Lots of fun for everyone!

Taking photos every day,
Making sand castles,
Hurray, hurray!

Summer, summer, summer fun,
Lots of fun for everyone!

**2** Look and say.

69

## LESSON 2

**3** Listen and read. 8.2

Sandra, do you like surfing?

No, I don't.

Do you like playing Frisbee®?

No, I don't.

Do you like making sand castles?

No, I don't.

Do you like eating ice cream?

Yes, I do.

Do you like chocolate or strawberry ice cream?

I like chocolate AND strawberry ice cream!

**4** Ask a friend.

1. Do you like making sand castles?
2. Do you like reading comics?
3. Do you like camping?
4. Do you like eating ice cream?
5. Do you like singing songs?
6. Do you like dancing?

LESSON 3

**5** Listen and say the number.

**6** Play three-in-a-row and say.

71

# Shark Attack!

**LESSON 4**

**7** Read and listen to the story.

# LESSON 5

**8** Listen and chant. 8.5

Do you like surfing?
Yes, I do! And I like taking photos too!

Do you like snorkeling in the sea?
No, I don't, that's not for me!

Do you like sailing?
Yes, I do! And I like eating ice cream too!

Do you like camping by the sea?
No, I don't, that's not for me!

**9** Play a game.

74

CLIL

LESSON 6

**10** Read and write the number.

A
B
C
D

1
In the summer, I go to the beach with my family. I like making sand castles and snorkeling.

2
In the summer, I go to the mountains with my dad. I like camping and eating hot dogs.

3
In the summer, I go to a water park with my friends. I like swimming and playing in the water.

4
In the summer, I go to an aquarium with my grandma. I like taking photos of the dolphins.

**11** Write about your favorite summer activities.

# Beep's World!

LITERACY

## LESSON 7

**12** Read and listen.

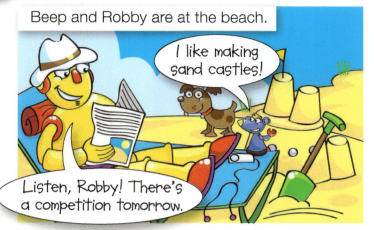

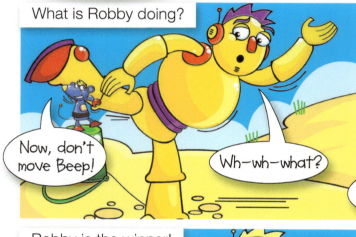

**13** Listen and repeat a tongue twister.

Sarah likes sailing,
And snorkeling too.
Sally likes surfing.
What about you?

**1** Read and say.

1. It's big and old, and it's orange and white.
2. It's new and fast.
3. It's old and fast, and it's red.
4. It's small and slow.

**2** Ask a friend.

1. Do you like sailing?
2. Do you like camping?
3. Do you like reading comics?
4. Do you like taking photos?
5. Do you like dancing?
6. Do you like surfing?

**3** Read and write about you.

Hello, my name's Eva. I'm nine. I like snorkeling and surfing. I don't like playing Frisbee®. My favorite sport is swimming. Bye!

# 3

## Activity Book

Richmond

# Contents

0 Hello!......2
1 Ready for School......3
2 Busy Morning!......5
3 Story World......7

4 Sports......9
5 Nature Park......11
6 After-School Fun!......13

7 Transportation......15
8 Summer Fun!......17
Picture Dictionary......19
Beep on Grammar......27
Track List......35

# Hello!

**1** Read, match and complete.

I'm   Karim   Lucy   nine   eight

I'm _____. I'm eight.

I'm _____. I'm eight.

I'm Olga. I'm _____.

__ Tom. I'm _____.

**2** Draw yourself and answer.

What's your name?
I'm _____.

How old are you?
I'm _____.

What's your favorite color?
It's _____.

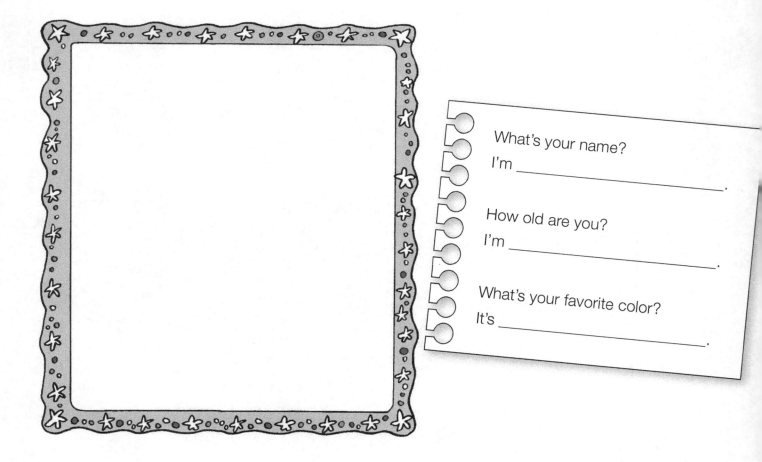

# 1. Ready for School

**1** Listen and put a checkmark (✓) or a cross (✗). 1.1

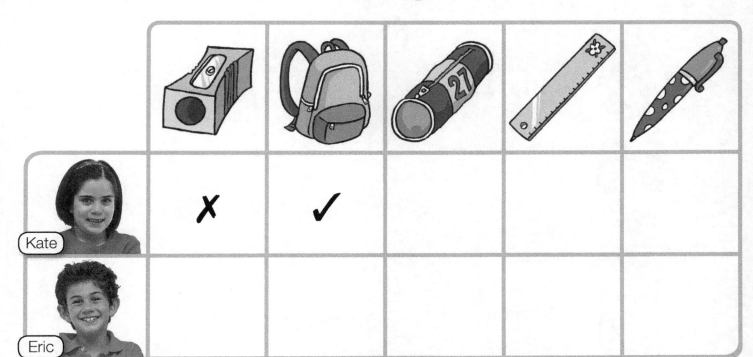

**2** Complete and write your answers.

✓ = Yes, I do.    ✗ = No, I don't.

1  Do you have a blue __ __ __?  _____

2  Do you have a __ __ __ __ __ __ __  __ __ __ __?  _____

3  Do you have a __ __ __ __ __?  _____

4  Do you have a yellow __ __ __ __ __ __? _____

5  Do you have a white __ __ __ __ __ __?  _____

6  Do you have a __ __ __ __ __ __ __ __?  _____

3

# Review

**1** Write the questions and circle your answers.

have you a dog? Do _____
Yes, I do.    No, I don't.

you Do bike? have a _____
Yes, I do.    No, I don't.

a have Do you computer? _____
Yes, I do.    No, I don't.

cat? have a you Do _____
Yes, I do.    No, I don't.

**2** Look at the chart and write.

It's + in  under + the books.   the apple.
      on  behind   the chair.   the pencil case.

1 _____.

2 _____.

3 _____.

4 _____.

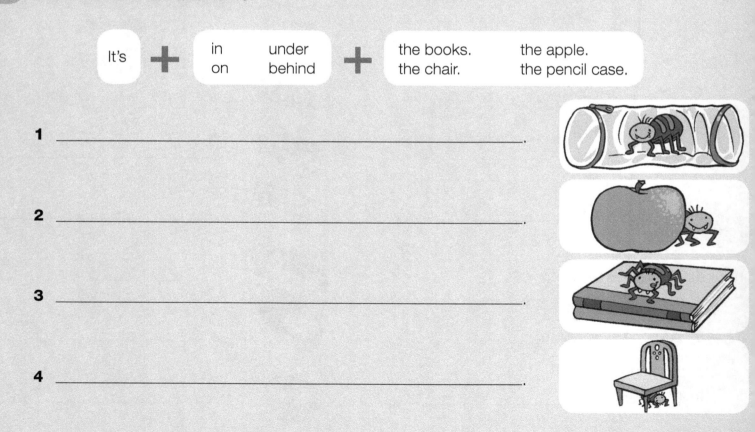

4

# 2. Busy Morning!

**1** Listen and draw the times.

**2** Write and circle.

> brush my teeth   have breakfast   go to school   get dressed

**1** I _____ at seven o'clock / nine o'clock.

**2** I _____ at ten thirty / eight thirty.

**3** I _____ at nine o'clock / ten o'clock.

**4** I _____ at five thirty / seven thirty.

# Review

**1** Look and match.

get
take a
brush my
get
have
go to

breakfast
dressed
up
shower
school
teeth

**2** Look and complete.

1 It's _____

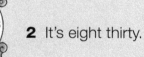

2 It's eight thirty.

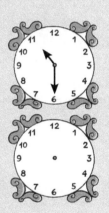

3 _____

4 It's seven o'clock.

**3** Cross out the extra letters and number the days in order.

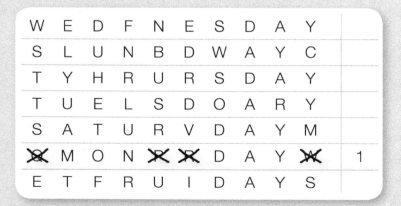

# 3. Story World

**1** Listen and number the characters.

**2** Look and write, then draw.

He's   She's

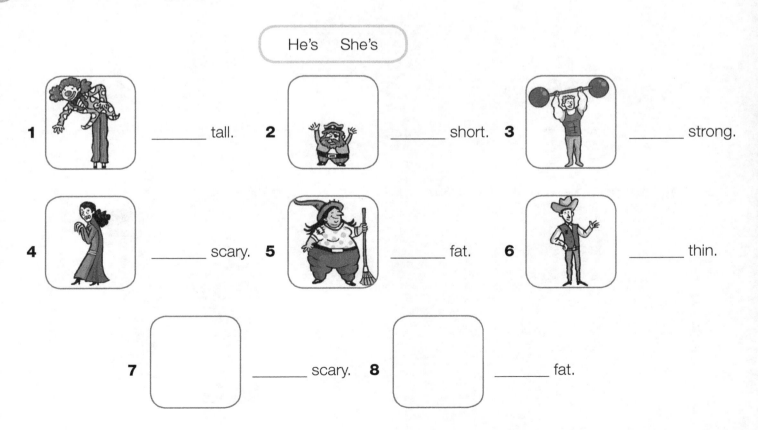

1 _____ tall.   2 _____ short.   3 _____ strong.

4 _____ scary.   5 _____ fat.   6 _____ thin.

7 _____ scary.   8 _____ fat.

7

# Review

**1** Look and complete.

1  p_ _nc_s_  2  _ _p_rh_r_  3  p_ _at_  4  d_ _ _o_

**2** Look and write.

_____   _____   _____

_____   _____   _____

**3** Look and complete with *His* or *Her*.

1  _____ name is Karim.
2  _____ cat is black.
3  _____ name is Lucy.
4  _____ nose is not scary.
5  _____ nose is scary.

# 4. Sports

**1** Listen and circle the faces. 4.1

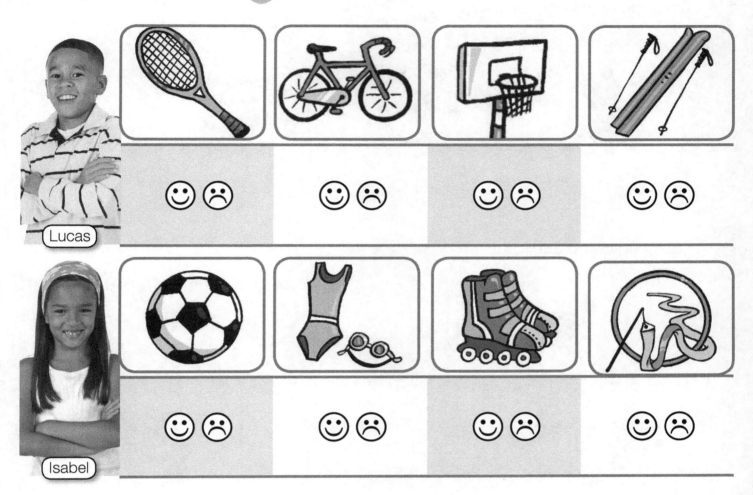

**2** Write in order and number.

like rollerblading doesn't He    _____.
gymnastics likes She    _____.
likes He basketball    _____.
doesn't skiing She like    _____.

# Review

**1** Write the names of the sports.

1 _____  2 _____  3 _____  4 _____

**2** Look and complete.

1 _____ riding a bike.

3 _____ skiing.

He / She

likes / doesn't like

2 _____ gymnastics.

4 _____ rollerblading.

**3** Look and write.

1 She _____.
2 _____.
3 _____.

1 He _____.
2 _____.
3 _____.

10

# 5. Nature Park

**1** Listen and number the animals.

**2** Complete the sentences.

It has ✓     It doesn't have ✗

1 _____ four legs.
2 _____ wings.
3 _____ a tail.

4 _____ a tail.
5 _____ six legs.
6 _____ claws.

7 It has _____.
8 It has _____.
9 It doesn't have _____.

11

# Review

**1** Look and complete.

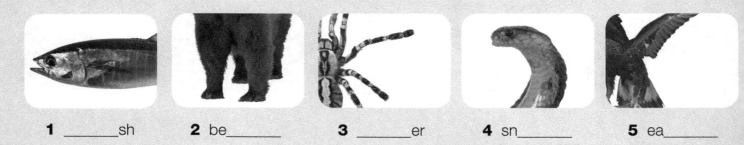

1 ____sh    2 be____    3 ____er    4 sn____    5 ea____

**2** Follow and circle the right word.

It has *wings / a tail*.

It has *two / four* legs.

It has *claws / wings*.

It has *wings / a tail*.

It has *six / eight* legs.

It has *a tail / legs*.

**3** Write the question and put a checkmark (✓) or a cross (✗).

lfy    1 Can it _____?

nur    2 ____ ____ _____?

licbm eetrs    3 ____ ____ _____ _____?

miws    4 ____ ____ _____?

12

# 6. After-School Fun!

**1** Listen and match. 6.1

**2** Look at Activity 1 and answer the questions.

1 What's Danny doing? _____
2 What's Anna doing? _____
3 What's Sally doing? _____
4 What's Tony doing? _____

**3** Correct the sentences.

1 She's gardening.        2 He's playing the guitar.        3 He's doing a puzzle.

_____    _____    _____

13

# Review

**1** Read, follow the lines and circle.

1 He's dancing.

2 She's gardening.

3 He's doing a puzzle.

4 She's reading.

True   False

True   False

True   False

True   False

**2** Look and answer.

1 What's Oscar doing?
   _____.

2 What's Naomi doing?
   _____.

3 What's Bill doing?
   _____.

**3** Write the rooms.

om / ba / ro / th        en / kit / ch        rd / en / ga        om / dro / be

_____        _____        _____        _____

14

# 7. Transportation

**1** Listen and color.

**2** Match and write.

ten
twenty
thirty
forty
fifty
sixty
seventy
eighty
ninety
a hundred

50    70    40
___   ___   ___

10    90    30    60
___   ___   ___   ___

100   20    80
___   ___   ___

# Review

**1** Look and write.

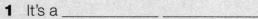
fast   car   new   plane   slow   plane   old   bike

1  It's a _____ _____          2  It's an _____ _____

3  It's a _____ _____          4  It's a _____ _____

**2** Look and complete.

1  f _ _ _ _ _ _

2 t h _ _ _ _ _ _

3 _ _ _ _ _ _ _ _ _

4 _ w _ _ _ _ _

**3** Look and write.

1  It's a _____.   2  It's _____.   3  _____

16

# 8. Summer Fun!

**1** Listen and draw. 8.1

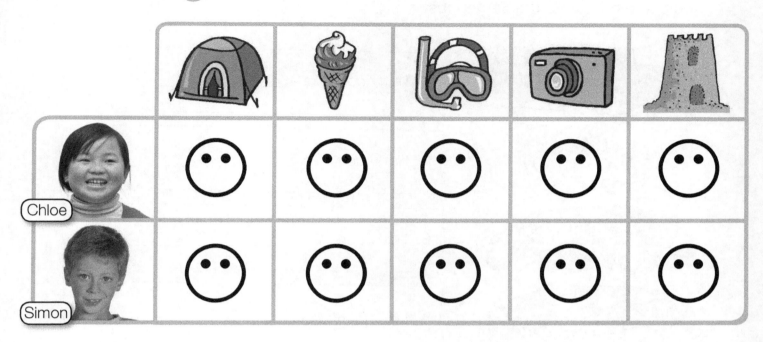

**2** Complete the sentences and answer *Yes, I do* or *No, I don't*.

eating    playing    singing    camping    dancing    playing

1  Do you like _____ Frisbee®? _____

2  Do you like _____? _____

3  Do you like _____ ice cream? _____

4  Do you like _____? _____

5  Do you like _____ tennis? _____

6  Do you like _____? _____

17

# Review

**1** Circle and complete the sentences.

1 I *like / don't like* _____.

2 I *like / don't like* _____.

3 I *like / don't like* _____.

4 I *like / don't like* _____.

**2** Look and complete.

| He | likes | playing Frisbee® | camping |
| She | doesn't like | surfing | snorkeling |

1 _____.

2 _____.

3 _____.

4 _____.

# Picture Dictionary 1

 books
_____

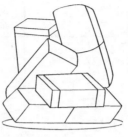 erasers
_____

 pencil cases
_____

 pencils
_____

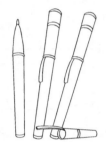 pens
_____

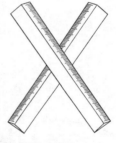 rulers
_____

 schoolbags
_____

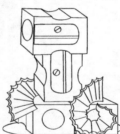 sharpeners
_____

 behind
_____

 in
_____

 on
_____

 under
_____

# Picture Dictionary 2

brush my teeth

get dressed

get up

go to school

have breakfast

take a shower

# Picture Dictionary 3

dragon

dwarf

giant

pirate

prince

princess

superhero

witch

# Picture Dictionary 4

basketball

_____

gymnastics

_____

riding a bike

_____

rollerblading

_____

skiing

_____

soccer

_____

swimming

_____

tennis

_____

# Picture Dictionary 5

bear
_____

butterfly
_____

eagle
_____

fish
_____

snake
_____

spider
_____

squirrel
_____

wolf
_____

claws
_____

legs
_____

tail
_____

wings
_____

23

# Picture Dictionary 6

 dancing

 doing puzzles

 gardening

 making models

 playing cards

 playing the guitar

 reading

 singing

# Picture Dictionary 7

 bike

 boat

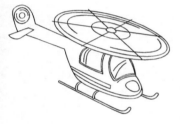 bus

 car

 helicopter

 hot-air balloon

 plane

 ship

 train

25

# Picture Dictionary 8

camping
_____

making sand castles
_____

sailing
_____

surfing
_____

eating ice cream
_____

playing Frisbee ®
_____

snorkeling
_____

taking photos
_____

26

# Beep on Grammar 1

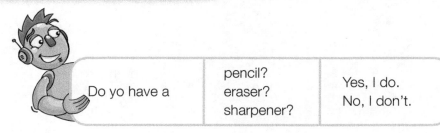

**1** Write the questions and answers.

1 Do you have a pencil ? ✓ Yes, I do .
2 _____ ? ✗ _____ .
3 _____ ? ✗ _____ .
4 _____ ? ✓ _____ .
5 _____ ? ✗ _____ .
6 _____ ? ✓ _____ .

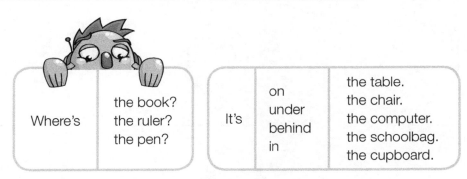

**2** Look and answer.

1 Where's the shoe? It's under the table.
2 Where's the cat? _____
3 Where's the computer? _____
4 Where's the soccer ball? _____
5 Where's the ruler? _____
6 Where's the schoolbag? _____

27

# Beep on Grammar 2

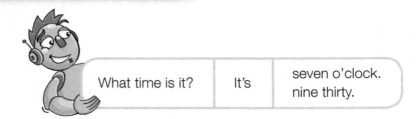

**1** Read and draw the time.

**1** It's eight o'clock.  **2** It's twelve thirty.  **3** It's seven thirty.  **4** It's three o'clock.

**2** Look and write the time.

1 _____    2 _____    3 _____

**3** Write sentences.

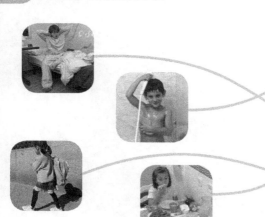

1 _____

2 _____

3 <u>I get up at six thirty.</u>

4 _____

# Beep on Grammar 3

|  | tall. |
|---|---|
| He's | short. |
| She's | fat. |
|  | thin. |
|  | strong. |
|  | scary. |

**1** Look and describe the characters.

1 _____
2 _____
3 _____
4 _____
5 _____
6 _____

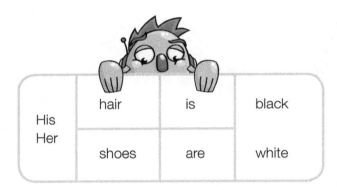

| | | | |
|---|---|---|---|
| His | hair | is | black |
| Her | shoes | are | white |

**2** Look and complete the sentences with *His* or *Her*.

1 _____ dog is black and white.
2 _____ nose is big.
3 _____ cat is gray.
4 _____ shoes are gray.
5 _____ nose is small.
6 _____ shoes are white.

29

# Beep on Grammar 4

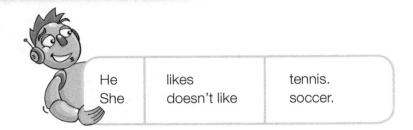

**1** Look at the chart and write sentences.

1  He likes swimming.
2  _____
3  _____
4  _____
5  _____
6  _____

**2** Look and write sentences.

1  He can play tennis.
2  _____
3  _____
4  _____
5  _____
6  _____

# Beep on Grammar 5

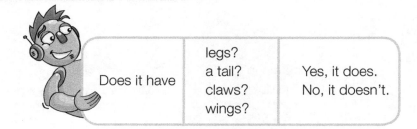

| Does it have | legs?<br>a tail?<br>claws?<br>wings? | Yes, it does.<br>No, it doesn't. |

**1** Write the questions and answer.

1  it / claws / have / Does ?
   _____Does it have claws?_____

 Yes, it does.    _____    _____

2  wings / it / Does / have ?
   _____

 _____

3  have / it / Does / a tail ?
   _____

 _____    _____    _____

| It has<br>It doesn't have | a tail.<br>wings.<br>legs.<br>claws. |

**2** Look and complete.

 1 _It has a tail._____    3 _____ six legs.    5 _____ claws.

 2 _____ wings.    4 _____ a tail.    6 _____ two legs.

# Beep on Grammar 6

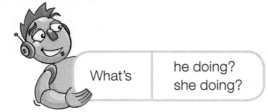

| What's | he doing?<br>she doing? | He's<br>She's | reading.<br>dancing.<br>doing puzzles. |

**1** Look, circle and answer.

1 What's **he** /(**she**) doing?

_She's gardening._

4 What's **he** / **she** doing?

_____

2 What's **he** / **she** doing?

_____

5 What's **he** / **she** doing?

_____

3 What's **he** / **she** doing?

_____

6 What's **he** / **she** doing?

_____

| Where's | Mom?<br>Dad?<br>Grandma? | She's<br>He's | in the car.<br>in the kitchen.<br>in the hall.<br>in the garden.<br>in the bathroom. |

**2** Look and complete.

1 Where's Karim? _He's in the garden._____

2 Where's Grandpa? _____

3 Where's Dad? _____

4 Where's Karim's sister? _____

5 Where's Beep? _____

32

# Beep on Grammar 7

It's   new and fast.
       old and slow.

**1** Look, unscramble and write.

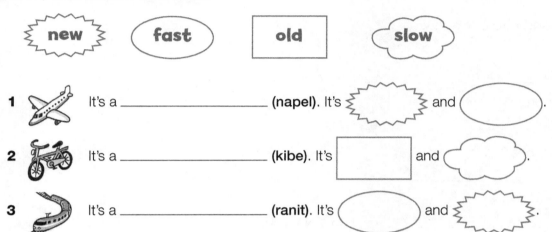

1  It's a _____ (napel). It's _____ and _____.
2  It's a _____ (kibe). It's _____ and _____.
3  It's a _____ (ranit). It's _____ and _____.

**2** Read. Draw and write.

It's a ship.
It's old and slow.

It's _____.
It's _____ and _____.

Is it  new?    Yes, it is.
       fast?   No, it isn't.

**3** Look and write the answers and the questions.

1  Is it fast?  ✓ _____
2  Is it slow?  ✗ _____

3  Is it old?   ✗ _____
4  Is it fast?  ✓ _____

5  _____Is it old_____? No, it isn't.
6  _____? Yes, it is.

7  _____? No, it isn't.
8  _____? Yes, it is.

33

# Beep on Grammar 8

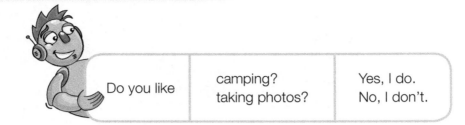

| Do you like | camping?<br>taking photos? | Yes, I do.<br>No, I don't. |

**1** Write the questions and circle for you.

you surfing Do like
1 ___Do you like surfing___? Yes, I do. / No, I don't.

you photos like Do taking
2 _____? Yes, I do. / No, I don't.

like Do playing you Frisbee ®
3 _____? Yes, I do. / No, I don't.

camping you Do like
4 _____? Yes, I do. / No, I don't.

playing you cards Do like
5 _____? Yes, I do. / No, I don't.

**2** Circle *like* or *don't like*.

In the morning, I like / don't like . I like / don't like .

On Saturdays, I like / don't like . I like / don't like .

In the summer, I like / don't like . I like / don't like .

# Track List

| | | **Student's Book** |
|---|---|---|
| | | **Songs, chants and stories** |

| Track | Transcript | |
|---|---|---|
| **Unit 0** | | |
| 1 | 0.1 | Song: What's your name? |
| 2 | 0.3 | Song: The Alphabet Song |
| 3 | 0.4 | Song: The Numbers Song |
| **Unit 1** | | |
| 4 | 1.1 | Song: Ready for School! |
| 5 | 1.4 | Story: A School Trip! |
| 6 | 1.5 | Chant: Where's the book? |
| 7 | 1.6 | Beep's World! |
| **Unit 2** | | |
| 8 | 2.1 | Song: Busy Morning! |
| 9 | 2.5 | Story: Lucy's New Watch! |
| 10 | 2.6 | Song: My Week |
| 11 | 2.7 | Beep's World! |
| **Unit 3** | | |
| 12 | 3.1 | Song: Come to Story World |
| 13 | 3.3 | Story: Sleeping Beauty! |
| 14 | 3.4 | Chant: Who is this? |
| 15 | 3.5 | Beep's World! |
| **Unit 4** | | |
| 16 | 4.1 | Song: Sports Are Great! |
| 17 | 4.4 | Story: School Field Day! |
| 18 | 4.5 | Chant: What can they do? |
| 19 | 4.6 | Beep's World! |
| **Unit 5** | | |
| 20 | 5.1 | Song: Come With Me |
| 21 | 5.3 | Story: Bear Attack! |
| 22 | 5.4 | Chant: A Fish Can Swim |
| 23 | 5.6 | Beep's World! |
| **Unit 6** | | |
| 24 | 6.1 | Song: After-School Fun! |
| 25 | 6.4 | Story: Where are they? |
| 26 | 6.5 | Chant: Where's Dad? |
| 27 | 6.6 | Beep's World! |

| Track | Transcript | |
|---|---|---|
| **Unit 7** | | |
| 28 | 7.1 | Song: Traveling |
| 29 | 7.4 | Story: The Lighthouse! |
| 30 | 7.5 | Chant: Little Racing Cars! |
| 31 | 7.7 | Beep's World! |
| **Unit 8** | | |
| 32 | 8.1 | Song: Summer Fun! |
| 33 | 8.4 | Story: Shark Attack! |
| 34 | 8.5 | Chant: Do you like surfing? |
| 35 | 8.6 | Beep's World! |

| | | **Activity Book** |
|---|---|---|
| | | **Exercises** |

| Track | Transcript | |
|---|---|---|
| 36 | 1.1 | Listen and put a checkmark (✓) or a cross (✗). |
| 37 | 2.1 | Listen and draw the times. |
| 38 | 3.1 | Listen and number the characters. |
| 39 | 4.1 | Listen and circle the faces. |
| 40 | 5.1 | Listen and number the animals. |
| 41 | 6.1 | Listen and match. |
| 42 | 7.1 | Listen and color. |
| 43 | 8.1 | Listen and draw. |

| | | **Picture Dictionary** |
|---|---|---|
| 44 | PD1 | Picture Dictionary 1 |
| 45 | PD2 | Picture Dictionary 2 |
| 46 | PD3 | Picture Dictionary 3 |
| 47 | PD4 | Picture Dictionary 4 |
| 48 | PD5 | Picture Dictionary 5 |
| 49 | PD6 | Picture Dictionary 6 |
| 50 | PD7 | Picture Dictionary 7 |
| 51 | PD8 | Picture Dictionary 8 |